EMOTIONAL HEALTH ISSUES

Abuse and Neglect

Sarah Medina

WAYLAND

HAVERING COLLEGE

LEARNING
RESOURCES
CENTRE

First published in 2008
by Wayland

Copyright © Wayland 2008

Wayland
Hachette Children's Books
338 Euston Road
London NW1 3BH

Wayland Australia
Level 17/207 Kent Street
Sydney, NSW 2000

Series editor: Nicola Edwards
Consultant: Peter Evans
Designer: Alix Wood
Picture researcher: Kathy Lockley

The case studies in this book are based on real experiences but the names we have used are fictitious and do not relate to real people. Except where a caption of a photograph describes an event in which real people have taken part, all the people we have featured in the book are models.

The author and publisher would like to thank the following for allowing their pictures to be reproduced in this publication:
G.M.B. Akash/Panos Pictures: 7b; John Angerson/Alamy: 16; Paul Baldesare/Photofusion: titlepage, 10; Emely/zefa/Corbis: 44; Randy Faris/Corbis: 8; Maurizio Gamberini/dpa/Corbis: 7t; Gianni Giansanti/Sygma/Corbis: 29 Kirsty-Anne Glubish/Design Pics/Corbis: 15; image100/Corbis: 11, 40; Image Source/Corbis: 17, 39; Le Studio/AgenceImage/Jupiterimages: 14; Lucidio Studio, Inc./Corbis: 35; Roy McMahon/Corbis: 4; Nonstock/JupiterImages: 34; Ulrike Preuss/Photofusion: Cover, 42; Ivy Reynolds/Botanica/Jupiterimages: 30; Benjamin Rondel/Corbis: 5; Sciencephotos/Alamy:18; Ian Scrivener/Alamy: 28; Wishlist: 9, 12, 20, 21, 23, 24, 25, 27, 31, 32, 33, 36, 38, 41, 43, 45

British Library Cataloguing in Publication Data
 Medina, Sarah
   Emotional, physical and sexual abuse. - (Emotional health
   issues)
   1. Child abuse - Juvenile literature
   I. Title
   362.7'6

ISBN: 978 0 7502 4914 0

Printed in China

Wayland is a division of Hachette Children's Books, an Hachette Livre UK company.

Contents

Words that appear in **bold** can be found in the
glossary on page 46.

Introduction

Brinda's boyfriend says she does everything wrong. He calls her fat, ugly and lazy, and he gets angry when she wants to spend time with her family and friends. Brinda feels lonely, trapped and miserable.

Every day, 14-year-old Carlos's parents hit him. He often has cuts and bruises, but he always finds an excuse to cover up what happened. Carlos is terrified; recently, his father tried to strangle him. Carlos feels worthless and spends all his time thinking about how he can end his life.

Laura, 18, was abused by her uncle when she was 12. He made her touch private parts of his body, and he touched her body inappropriately. He told Laura the touching was 'their secret' and threatened to hurt her if she told anyone. Laura has never had a boyfriend; she still feels ashamed, and she is afraid that men are going to hurt her.

Omar lives alone and he needs help with personal care. His son's wife agreed to help him but, some days, she does not come until lunchtime. Omar is left in bed, feeling hungry and uncomfortable. Omar does not tell his son; he does not want to burden him. Every night, he goes to sleep hoping that he will not wake up again in the morning.

Abuse can take many forms. Within a relationship, physical abuse may be combined with emotional abuse and can cause anxiety, fear and unhappiness.

Elderly people who may be physically frail and lacking in confidence are particularly vulnerable to abusive behaviour.

their age, wealth, education, religion or family circumstances. Some people – such as elderly or ill individuals, people with **disabilities** and children – are seen as 'easy' targets for abusers.

What is abuse?

Abuse is cruel and hurtful treatment towards a person. There are four main types of abuse. **Emotional abuse**, as in Brinda's case, damages a person's feelings. **Physical abuse** attacks someone's body, like Carlos's. **Sexual abuse** is sexual contact that is forced on someone, like Laura. **Neglect**, as in Omar's case, is a form of abuse that involves ignoring someone's physical or emotional needs.

Abuse can occur just about anywhere: at home, school or work; in institutions, such as care homes; and out and about in the community. And abuse can be carried out by just about anyone, even by those who should give love and care, such as family, friends and partners.

Abuse has no barriers. It damages, and even threatens, the lives of millions of people all over the world, no matter

Find out more

This book focuses on the effects of abuse on children and young people. The first chapter deals with children's rights and needs. Later sections cover the four main forms of abuse. Finally, there is advice on how to find help to stop abuse from happening and how people can be supported in recovering from abuse and neglect.

It's a fact: child abuse

- According to the World Health Organization, approximately 40 million children in all parts of the world suffer child abuse each year.

Chapter 1: Children's rights and children's needs

Everyone deserves to be treated well. Governments make laws to ensure that people's rights are protected. There are laws to protect children's rights, too. It is good to know what our rights are. This helps us to be clear about what is – and is not – good behaviour towards us.

The UN Convention on the Rights of the Child

Many children's rights have been agreed internationally. The United Nations (UN) Convention on the Rights of the Child is one of the most important international agreements for children. It is a list of 54 rights that children should have. So far, more than 190 countries, including the UK and United States, have signed the Convention. This means that those countries look at the Convention when they make laws to protect children.

What does the UN Convention say?

The UN Convention on the Rights of the Child covers many areas of life that may involve children, including school, work and play. It starts by setting out the most basic right of all: that children have the right to life.

In focus: whose rights?

The UN Convention on the Rights of the Child says that everyone under the age of 18 has all the rights listed in the Convention. The Convention applies to everyone, whatever their race, religion or abilities, whatever they think or say, and whatever type of family they come from.

It then goes on to list the other rights that children should have to make their lives better.

Some parts of the UN Convention deal directly with the issue of child abuse and neglect. For example, the Convention says that governments should protect children from violence, abuse and neglect by their parents or

It's a fact:
the UN Convention on the Rights of the Child

The Convention makes it clear that:

- Children have the right to good-quality health care, to clean water and nutritious food, and to a clean environment, so that they will stay healthy.

- Children have a right to an education.

- All children have a right to relax and play, and to join in different activities.

- Parents should always consider what is best for each of their children.

- Governments should protect children from work that might hurt them in any way.

by anyone else who looks after them. Governments should also protect children from sexual abuse and from dangerous drugs.

The problem of child abuse needs to be wiped out. The UN Convention is helping to do this. It has already helped millions of children by making sure that governments know about and protect the rights of young people.

Some children are forced to work, often in terrible conditions. This is child abuse.

Children's needs

Children have needs – both physical and emotional – as well as rights. It is the responsibility of parents and caregivers to look after children's needs. When their needs are ignored, children suffer.

Physical needs

A child's most basic physical needs are food and drink. Children who have nothing to eat will die in weeks. Without a drink, they will die in days. Children also need a safe place to live and clothes to wear. Good health care helps to keep children well, and supervision helps to keep them safe.

Emotional needs

Children need love and care just as much as they need food and drink. A warm, secure home life helps

children to develop good **self-esteem**. Children who feel unloved or insecure feel bad about themselves. This makes it harder for them to be happy and to do well in life.

Children need time and attention from their parents or caregivers, so they know that they are loved and special. Respect helps them to

Spending time together as a family makes children feel loved and valued.

Alcohol can make some people aggressive. But drinking too much is never an excuse for abusive behaviour.

feel sure about themselves. Praise and encouragement make them want to succeed and to behave well. Guidance and appropriate **discipline** teach them right from wrong. And reassurance when things go wrong helps them to feel safe.

Why does abuse happen?

There are many reasons why people abuse others. Some people who were abused when they were young may abuse their own children. They may think that abuse is 'normal' behaviour. Other people simply are unable to control themselves when they get angry, and they lash out at the people around them.

Stress can cause some people to be abusive. If people are unhappy, they may not think about how they are making others unhappy. Or they may behave badly because they are abusing alcohol or other drugs.

Recognizing abuse

Sometimes, people do not realize that they are being abused. Knowing our rights and needs helps us to recognize abuse. See page 38 for information about how to put a stop to abuse.

In focus: any excuse?

There may be a reason why someone abuses someone else, but there is never an excuse. Abusers are completely responsible for what they do. Abuse is never the child's fault – and abuse is always wrong.

Chapter 2: *Emotional abuse*

Emotional abuse occurs when someone attacks the feelings of another person. It is sometimes called psychological abuse, mental abuse or verbal abuse. Emotional abuse is often carried out through words. It affects the way people think about themselves, as well as their feelings. Emotional abuse may not leave any outward physical scars, but it can leave very deep and long-lasting scars within.

What is emotional abuse?

Adults can be hurt by emotional abuse. People who are unhappy in a relationship may emotionally abuse their partners by yelling at or insulting each other. **Domestic violence** often involves emotional abuse (see page 14). People with disabilities or people from **ethnic minorities** are abused emotionally when people insult them or treat them inconsiderately.

Children are **vulnerable** to emotional abuse, particularly when they witness violence between adults in the home. Children need a lot of love, care and respect to feel safe and confident as they grow up. When their parents or caregivers hurt them emotionally, they often feel worthless and confused. These feelings can last a lifetime.

Children who are emotionally abused at home may also be abused in other

When people are emotionally abused, they can feel very lost and lonely.

ways, too. For example, some parents may 'punish' their child in several different ways. They may emotionally abuse her by screaming at her that she is useless and shouting that they do not love her. They may threaten that the child's behaviour will make them ill or lead to their death and tell the child that this is all her fault. At the same time, they may physically abuse her by hitting or kicking her. They may then lock her in a room and ignore her, refusing to give her anything to eat or drink. That kind of treatment is neglect. These parents may think that they are simply being strict and teaching their child a lesson, but these behaviours are abusive – and wrong.

In focus: *how far is too far?*

Most people have arguments at some time. Family members sometimes get annoyed with one another. At school, children often fall out with one another. Anger is a normal feeling – but it is important that anger does not hurt anyone else. If someone's anger makes another person feel afraid or bad about themselves, this is emotional abuse.

CASE STUDY

Lolly's parents adore her older sister, Tanya. They buy Tanya lots of things and spend time with her, taking her to eat out or to the cinema. But they pay little attention to Lolly. They often leave her at home when they take Tanya out, saying that she has to do her homework or clean her room. Although Lolly tries really hard to be 'good', her parents make her feel that no one will ever love her. Lolly has no self-confidence, and she is struggling to keep up at school. She feels very lonely and unhappy.

How is emotional abuse carried out?

Emotional abuse can come in many forms, from ignoring someone to calling him or her names, from not caring at all to demanding too much. These ways of behaving may seem **contradictory**, but they are all ways in which people emotionally abuse others.

Humiliating people by laughing at them is not funny. It is a form of emotional abuse which can make people feel isolated and vulnerable.

Shouting and frightening

Shouting is a common form of emotional abuse. We have seen that anger is a normal feeling. However, anger can **intimidate** people, especially children. Many abusers want to frighten their victims. They may threaten to hurt them or to leave them. They may damage their victims' belongings or attack their pets.

Criticizing and humiliating

Abusers often make themselves feel better by making others feel terrible through constant criticism. They may insult their victims by saying that they do everything wrong or that no one cares about them. They may blame their victims when things go wrong. They may **humiliate** people by calling them names or by teasing. Abusers may say that they are 'only joking' – but emotional abuse is not a joke.

It's a fact: working children

- In developing countries, more than 120 million children aged between five and 14 work full-time, according to the organization Human Rights Watch.

Withdrawing love and attention

Emotional abuse can sometimes be more about what the abuser does not do than what he or she does do. Some abusers refuse to show love to their victims. They may be cold towards a child or another family member. Abusers may refuse to spend time with their victims. These types of behaviour leave children feeling completely **rejected**. Often, that outcome is exactly what the abuser wants.

Isolating

Locking a child in a room is a way to isolate him or her – and it is another form of emotional abuse. An abuser can feel very powerful by taking away a victim's right to be with other people. Isolation can also happen when the abuser stops the victim from seeing friends or taking part in activities outside school.

Demanding

Sometimes people expect too much of others. An abusive parent may demand that a daughter gets straight As in all her exams. A parent may expect a child to study all the time, even when she is tired, or may demand that she does housework every day. Victims of demanding behaviour often feel that they have to do everything perfectly.

Corrupting

Some people emotionally abuse others by **corrupting** them – that is, by encouraging unacceptable or harmful behaviour. Some parents may allow their children to use drugs or alcohol. They may ask their children to do things that are illegal, such as stealing, or they may encourage fighting with other children.

Exploiting

Exploitation occurs when someone unfairly uses or forces someone else to do something for them. In some countries, children are forced to work

CASE STUDY

Aatmaja, who is 11 years old, works in a factory in India. She starts work at four o'clock in the morning and works 12 hours a day. Her work is exhausting, and the factory is dirty and noisy. Aatmaja has not got a bedroom – or even a bed. She is forced to sleep on the grimy factory floor, between the heavy machines. She only has rice to eat, and she has to pay her boss for this. Aatmaja only gets to see her family once a week, and she misses them dreadfully. She dreams of living at home and going to school.

People often believe that domestic violence only involves adults. But children who see their parents or caregivers lashing out at each other can be very scared and worried.

from a very young age, perhaps to pay family debts. They often live away from their families, working as servants or in factories. Some children are even forced to fight in wars.

Domestic violence and children

In some families, domestic violence between parents or caregivers is a day-to-day reality for children.

Children may hear or witness emotional or physical abuse between adults they love. They may even try to step in to stop the abuse happening. This is a distressing and harmful form of emotional abuse for children.

In focus: *is bullying emotional abuse?*

When people think of bullying, they often think of physical abuse, such as pushing or hitting. However, bullying is often a form of emotional abuse, too – especially when the bully uses words to attack the victim's feelings. (See page 22 for more information about bullying.)

Emotional abusers

People who emotionally abuse others are often those we live, study or work with. They are usually people we expect to love or care for us. Most people who emotionally abuse others are older, bigger or stronger than their victims. They are often in a position of power, such as a parent over a child, or a teacher over a pupil.

Why do abusers do it?

Some parents find it difficult to accept their children as they are. Other parents have trouble dealing with the normal ups and downs of family life. They may be stressed, for example, if they are divorced or unemployed, and find it hard to control their feelings. They may have experienced abuse in their own childhoods which they have not recovered from. Older children may abuse their younger siblings because they are jealous of them. Some abusers have mental health problems, such as **depression**. They find it hard to respect the rights and needs of others. Others may be affected by alcohol or drugs.

Sometimes, people emotionally abuse others on purpose, because they want to control what their victim feels or does. Some emotional abuse is not deliberate – for example, a parent yelling at a child in a moment of **stress**. Often, people who emotionally abuse others blame their victim or make excuses for their behaviour. It is important to remember that there is never an excuse for emotional abuse.

Emotional abuse can come from people we really care about – even our boyfriends and girlfriends.

What are the effects of emotional abuse?

Long-term emotional abuse is deeply damaging. It makes people feel unloved and unimportant. Even one insult can hurt someone for many years. The effects of abuse may not be visible, but they are very serious.

Sadness and depression

Victims of emotional abuse usually feel very sad. They may hate themselves and become depressed. Life can seem hopeless. Depression may cause them to fall behind at school and withdraw from friends and fun activities.

Constant anxiety

Emotional abuse is very stressful. Because abusers are more powerful than their victims, victims often feel fear and loss of control. Some victims run away from home – sometimes more than once – because they cannnot cope anymore.

Anger and aggression

Victims often feel angry, which can make them act aggressively. Antisocial behaviour, such as lying or stealing, may become a problem.

Self-harm

Victims may feel so unhappy that they **self-harm** – for example, by abusing alcohol or drugs. Some people may engage in high-risk activities, such as driving too fast, which can indicate that

Some people are so desperate to feel relief from the agony of emotional abuse that they cut their arms so that they bleed.

Emotional abuse can make it hard for people to sleep, as the worry and fear go round and round in their mind.

It's a fact:

suicide

- In 2002 in England and Wales, 11 boys and 12 girls under the age of 14 died by suicide, according to a major mental health charity in the UK.
- According to a leading UK helpline, approximately 19,000 young people attempt suicide every year. That is one suicide attempt every 30 minutes.
- Suicide is the third leading cause of death for young people around the world, according to the World Health Organization.

their self-esteem is low and they do not respect themselves or others. Some victims cut themselves or harm their bodies in other ways. Some attempt **suicide** – and, sadly, some succeed.

Getting help

No one should have to suffer emotional abuse. It is important to know that help is available for victims. (See Getting Help, page 38.)

17

Chapter 3: *Physical abuse*

Physical abuse occurs when someone hurts another person's body in some way, either causing, or having the potential to cause, injury. Injury can be caused by a range of actions, from pushing or hitting to poisoning a person. Some injuries are very serious. In fact, physical abuse can – and does – lead to death. But all injuries, including cuts and bruises that heal within a few days, are serious. No one deserves to be hurt in this way.

What is physical abuse?

People who physically abuse others may commit other forms of abuse, too. For example, children who are emotionally abused (see page 10) may also be physically hurt. An older brother may kick a younger sibling while calling her stupid and useless. A school bully may shove a victim while laughing and calling the person

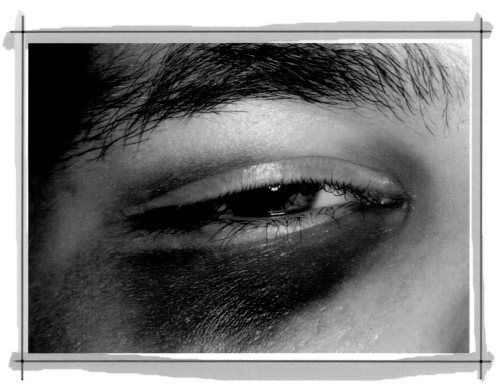

A black eye caused by physical abuse is not only painful to someone's body – it also causes deep emotional pain.

In focus: is smacking OK?

For many years, people have argued over the right of parents to smack their children. Is smacking physical abuse, or is it an acceptable way for parents to discipline their children?

Sweden was the first country to make smacking illegal. In 2005, England and Wales brought in laws to protect children. Parents who smack children so hard that it leaves a mark can be sent to prison for up to five years. In the United States, each state makes its own laws on **corporal punishment**. Many states allow parents to use 'reasonable' physical force to discipline their children.

People who support smacking say that it is a useful way for parents to discipline their children and that parents have the right to choose. Opponents argue that smacking is a form of physical abuse. They believe that it should be just as wrong to hit a child as it is to hit an adult.

names. Adults may use physical abuse to frighten and control children they are sexually abusing (see page 26).

Often, physical abuse is something that happens regularly, over a period of time. Some young people suffer physical abuse throughout their whole childhood. Sometimes, physical abuse happens during a stressful period – perhaps for a few weeks or a few months. But even a single incident of physical abuse – having hair pulled by a bully, or being kicked by a parent or caregiver, for example – can have long-lasting effects. Physical abuse is always a shock to the body, feelings and thoughts of the victim.

CASE STUDY

Donna's father was drunk when he grabbed her and pushed her against the kitchen wall. He yelled into Donna's face that she was lazy and stupid, because she did not have a drink waiting for him when he got home. Donna was terrified. Her hand was trapped and twisted hard behind her back. For days afterwards, her wrist was so swollen that she could hardly pick up her pen to do her schoolwork. It was very painful. And yet Donna did not tell anyone about her father's actions; she was too ashamed and she did not want to get him into trouble.

What does physical abuse involve?

People physically abuse others in many ways. Some actions, such as suffocating, are extreme and obviously life-threatening. Others, such as pushing or shoving, may seem less serious, but they are equally dangerous. A shove that results in a fall and a blow to the head can cause serious injury or even death.

Pushing or shaking

Pushing and shaking may not seem serious, but both actions are forms of physical abuse. People who are pushed may fall and hurt themselves badly. Shaking a baby or a small child can cause brain damage. Permanent disability or even death can occur.

Pinching, biting or hair-pulling

Some abusers pinch their victims, causing bruising or bleeding. Some bite, **puncturing** the skin and sometimes causing an infection. Others pull their victims' hair, sometimes hard enough to pull it out.

Hitting and beating

Hitting is a common form of physical abuse. Some abusers slap their victims with an open hand; others punch with their fist. Some abusers use objects, such as a wooden spoon or a rock, to beat their victims. Hitting and beating can cause injuries such as cuts, bruises and swelling. A black eye can result from being hit on the head.

Slapping someone across the face is shocking, hurtful – and unacceptable.

Kicking and throwing

A single kick to the foot or leg can be very painful. When an abuser keeps on kicking, especially at the head or face, serious harm can be caused, including the loss of an eye. Some abusers grab their victims and throw them against a door or a wall or onto the floor before kicking them.

Cutting and stabbing

Using knives to cut people is a dangerous form of physical abuse. Stabbing can be life-threatening, especially when an internal organ, such as the heart or liver, is pierced. Stabbing can cause people to bleed to death.

Picking on someone who uses a wheelchair and pushing or shoving that person is abusive behaviour that combines bullying with physical abuse. It takes advantage of the wheelchair user's physical vulnerability.

It's a fact:
physical punishment

- According to the World Health Organization, more than 80 per cent of children in many countries across the world suffer physical punishment in their homes.
- One-third of them experience severe physical punishment, caused by objects.
- The United Nations reports that 90 per cent of all children in the United Kingdom and the United States are physically punished during childhood.

CASE STUDY

Thirteen-year-old Antonio has to go to school by bus every day. Every morning, he dreads going to the bus stop. He knows that a group of older boys will be waiting to bully him. They began picking on him weeks ago. They started by calling him names and laughing at him. More recently, they have been pushing him around. They have grabbed his school bag and emptied it out all over the pavement. Antonio is afraid that things are going to get even worse. He is scared that the bullies are going to beat him up.

Poisoning

Some people physically abuse their victims by **poisoning** them. Most cases of poisoning happen to children under the age of three. They may be poisoned with alcohol or other drugs. Some victims are poisoned with salt. Too much salt can cause serious illness, brain damage and death.

Burning or scalding

Victims of physical abuse may be scarred permanently by burns from a cigarette, an iron, a hot stove or a flame. Some abusers scald young victims by placing them in a bath of extremely hot water. Victims of burning or scalding usually need to have their injuries treated at a hospital. Severe burns can sometimes lead to death.

Choking, drowning or suffocating

When victims are choked, drowned or suffocated, they are unable to breathe. Choking happens when an abuser puts his or her hands around a victim's neck to strangle the person. Drowning occurs when a victim's head is held underwater. Suffocation can occur when a victim's mouth and nose are covered and he or she is unable to breathe.

Bullying

Bullying happens all over the world – at home, at school and even at work. Some adults bully other adults, but bullying often occurs between children. Bullies use emotional abuse, such as name-calling, to make their victims feel bad about themselves. Bullies may physically abuse others, pushing, hitting or kicking them to cause fright. Bullying can be a terrifying experience. It is not 'just' bullying – it is abuse, and it is unacceptable.

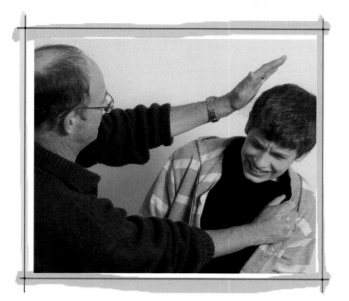

Hitting someone on the head can cause a lot of fear and stress and can also lead to a serious head injury.

Who carries out physical abuse?

Physical abuse is often carried out by people who are close to the victim. These include parents, siblings, boyfriends and girlfriends. Some caregivers physically abuse vulnerable people they look after, such as elderly or ill individuals, or people with disabilities.

Why do people abuse others?

Parents and caregivers do not always believe that their actions are physical abuse. They may think that hitting their children is an acceptable form of discipline.

Stress or depression can lead to physical abuse. Some people struggle to cope as they look after children or care for elderly relatives. People with personal problems, such as divorce or unemployment, sometimes physically abuse others to feel in control. Alcohol or other drugs may also be a factor.

Many people use physical abuse to control others. Girls who refuse to have sex with their boyfriends may be physically abused to make them **comply**. Some people cannot control their moods or tempers. Some people who were abused as children believe that abuse is normal.

There may be reasons why people physically abuse others — but there is never an excuse for it.

CASE STUDY

When 12-year old Miranda's friends started to smoke cigarettes, Miranda went along with them, just to be 'cool'. One day, Miranda's mother found some cigarettes in Miranda's clothes drawer – and she was furious. She yelled at Miranda and slapped her hard across her face and body. Since then, she has hit Miranda repeatedly. Miranda is shocked at her mother's behaviour. She doesn't understand why she is acting that way, and she is scared that her mother no longer loves her

What are the effects of physical abuse?

Physical abuse can lead to serious physical injury. Thousands of children die every year from injuries caused by physical abuse. Physical abuse affects more than the body, however. Victims suffer deep emotional scars, which heal much more slowly than physical damage.

Physical injury

Injuries caused by physical abuse vary a lot. Pushing, hitting and kicking can cause cuts, bruises, black eyes and broken bones and teeth. Some abusers pull their victim's hair so hard that it comes out. A knife stab can damage internal organs, such as kidneys. Shaking and poisoning can cause brain damage, and burns often leave permanent scars. Many forms of physical abuse can lead to death.

Stress, anxiety and fear

Many victims of physical abuse experience a great deal of stress. They worry constantly about when they might be abused next. Even though abuse is never the victim's fault, he or she may watch every move they make, afraid to set off another attack. Many have nightmares or cannot sleep. Their schoolwork may suffer because they are so tired.

Social problems

Victims of physical abuse may find it hard to trust people or form friendships. Some victims feel very angry and take out their rage on other people. They may become bullies, or get involved with lying or stealing.

When people are coping with physical abuse, they may not be able to cope with school as well. Then they feel even more alone.

24

Case Study

Mia's parents always find fault with her. They often find excuses to smack and punch her. In the past, they have broken Mia's glasses and have given her a black eye, but they frequently hit Mia's head, so that no one can see her injuries. Mia is desperately unhappy. She has tried running away from home several times, but she always ends up going back. She is afraid to talk to people about her experiences because she thinks that they will laugh at her. Mia does not want to die, but she feels that the only way out of the abuse is to kill herself.

People who are being physically abused may turn to alcohol in response to the desperation they feel.

Getting help

No one should have to suffer physical abuse. It is important to remember that help is available for victims of physical abuse. (See Getting Help, page 38.)

Low self-esteem

Physical abuse often makes victims feel ashamed and humiliated. They believe that they are worthless and that no one will ever love them. Low self-esteem like this can develop into severe depression and may last a lifetime.

Some victims of physical abuse try to escape abuse by attempting suicide. Others attempt to ease the emotional pain of abuse by self-harming. They may cut themselves or hurt their body in other ways.

It's a fact: physical abuse

- Worldwide in 2000, about 57,000 children between the ages of five and 14 died as a result of physical abuse.
- According to the World Health Organization, head injury is the most common cause of death.

Chapter 4: *Sexual abuse*

Sexual abuse occurs when someone is forced or **coerced** by others into sexual acts or situations. Sexual abuse can happen to children as well as adults. Sexual abusers often use physical abuse (see page 18) or emotional abuse (see page 10) to make their victim do what they want.

What is sexual abuse?

There are three main types of sexual abuse: non-touching sexual abuse, sexual touching and sexual exploitation. Any sexual contact between an adult and a child, or between an older child and a younger child, is sexual abuse. Sexual abuse can also take place within dating relationships between people of similar ages.

In non-touching sexual abuse, a person may force a victim to look at sexual parts of the abuser's body or to watch sexual acts. Some sexual abusers force their victims to look at sexual images or videos, called **pornography**. They may talk to their victims about sexual things in a way that is frightening or embarrassing.

A person who is kissed or touched in a sexual way against his or her wishes is also being sexually abused. This is true if the victim is made to kiss or touch

It's a fact: sexual abuse

- Every year, more than one million children worldwide are sexually exploited. They are forced to become prostitutes, sold for sexual purposes or used in child pornography, according to the United Nations.

- Experts say that approximately 20 per cent of women and 5 to 10 per cent of men worldwide suffered sexual abuse as children.

- Worldwide, in 2002, 150 million girls and 73 million boys under the age of 18 experienced rape or another form of sexual abuse.

someone else sexually, too. Rape occurs when sexual intercourse is forced on someone.

Sexual exploitation happens when a sexual abuser forces someone to have sexually **explicit** photographs taken of them. Some sexual abusers make sexual videos involving children. Others force children to become **prostitutes**. A prostitute has sexual contact with people in exchange for money.

All forms of sexual abuse are very serious – and illegal. Sexual abuse can be terrifying, especially for children, and it is extremely damaging to victims. It is impossible to forget. It can take victims many years to recover from sexual abuse.

CASE STUDY

Dan, aged 19, had been dating Rachel, aged 15, for four months. Rachel thought that she was in love with Dan. He seemed nice and they had a lot of fun. Rachel enjoyed kissing Dan, but she was not ready to have sexual intercourse. Dan said that he did not mind, and promised that he would wait. Then, one night, he drove Rachel to a secluded place, where he raped her. Rachel's world fell apart. She started to miss classes and to fall behind with her schoolwork. She did not want to see her friends, and she avoided spending time with her family. Rachel felt deeply ashamed. She thought it was her fault that Dan had raped her.

Being with a relative who wants to carry out sexual abuse is very frightening.

In focus: sex and the law

Many countries have laws to protect children and young people from sexual abuse and exploitation. In Great Britain and the United States, it is illegal for anyone to have any kind of sexual relationship with a child under the age of 16.

What does sexual abuse involve?

Sexual abuse includes non-touching sexual abuse, touching in a sexual way and sexual exploitation. Children may be abused in any of these ways. Sexual abuse can cause serious injury and even death.

Non-touching sexual abuse

Non-touching sexual abuse involves looking at the private parts of someone's body without their consent.

Indecent exposure occurs when the abuser exposes himself or herself to a victim. Some sexual abusers spy on children who are dressing or bathing. Others force their victims to undress in front of them.

Talking about sexual things is also a form of non-touching sexual abuse. Abusers may make sexual comments to their victim, or make them listen to stories that involve sex. Some abusers use email or text messages to send sexual suggestions to their victims.

Sexual abusers sometimes send sexually explicit text messages to their victims which are shocking and distressing to receive.

Pornography is sexually explicit material, including pictures and words. Sexual abusers may force their victims to look at pornographic magazines, photographs or films. Sometimes, victims are forced to watch other people in sexual situations.

Sexual touching

Touching forms of sexual abuse include kissing. Kissing may be on the mouth or body. Sexual abusers may touch intimate parts of the victim's body.

Sometimes, victims are made to touch the abuser's body. They may have to touch their own body while the abuser watches. Victims may also be forced to have sexual intercourse. This is rape. Rape can seriously injure the victim and lead to pregnancy.

Sexual exploitation

Some sexual abusers force their victims, including children, to become prostitutes. They are made to have sexual contact with people in exchange for money. They then have to give the money to their abuser.

Others force their victims into pornography. Child pornography includes sexually explicit photographs or films of children. Abusers may view child pornography themselves, or give or sell it to other sexual abusers.

Some young people are forced to become prostitutes against their will. They are too terrified to say no.

In focus: sex play or abuse?

When young people start dating, they may want to find out more about one another's bodies. Curiosity and exploration in the form of sex play are a normal part of growing up. Sex play is not the same as sexual abuse. Sexual abuse makes people feel uncomfortable, confused or afraid.

Dating is a healthy and fun part of growing up, but dating should always be about care for the other person, not control. If a boyfriend or girlfriend tries to make their partner engage in sexual activity before that person feels ready, this is sexual abuse – and it is wrong.

Dating and sexual abuse

Sexual abuse sometimes happens when people are dating. Some people mistake abuse for love. They may even find the attention flattering. However, sexual abuse is not about love – it is about control. Love involves care and respect.

Warning signs of sexual abuse within a relationship include any kind of unwanted sexual advances. Expressions such as 'If you loved me, you would...' are also warnings. People should always follow their instincts about a situation – if something does not feel right, it isn't.

CASE STUDY

John, aged 13, is scared to be around his uncle. Whenever Uncle Stan comes to visit, he tries to find ways to be alone with John. When they are alone, Uncle Stan talks a lot about sex, which makes John feel really uncomfortable. At times, John has noticed his uncle watching him, which feels creepy. On a couple of occasions, Uncle Stan has 'accidentally' walked into John's bedroom when John is in bed. John does not tell his parents because he is worried that they will not believe him. He thinks that his parents will believe Uncle Stan, because Uncle Stan is an adult.

Who carries out sexual abuse?

A common image of a sexual abuser is a creepy adult in a raincoat hanging around in a park. Most sexual abusers do not fit this image. They may be respected members of the community, such as religious leaders or teachers. They may be childcare professionals. Many sexual abusers are men, but women can be sexually abusive, too.

Although strangers sometimes carry out sexual abuse, most victims know and trust their abusers. An abuser may be a friend, a neighbour or a family member, such as a parent, sibling, grandparent or cousin. Sexual abuse may happen just once, or it may continue for a long time. It usually happens in private.

Why do some people abuse others?

Some people who were sexually abused when they were young grow up to abuse others. They may not know how to have a loving

If an adult pays 'special' attention to a younger individual that is inappropriate, it may be a sign that they want to sexually abuse them.

relationship. Some abusers, called **paedophiles**, find children sexually attractive. They may target children to feel more powerful and in control.

Sexual abusers may feel stressed or inadequate. They may abuse alcohol or other drugs. Sexual abuse is often about power and control. It is never about love. And, although there may be reasons why people sexually abuse others, there is never an excuse.

What are the effects of sexual abuse?

Even a single incident of sexual abuse can have serious and long-lasting effects on victims. Sexual abuse deeply damages a victim's self-esteem and it hurts his or her relationships with other people.

Shame and confusion

People often feel ashamed after experiencing sexual abuse. They may feel 'dirty', and keep washing themselves to 'wash away' what happened. Sexual abuse can be very confusing, too. Abusers may say that they love their victims and that the abuse is 'normal'. Some abusers accuse their victims of 'asking for' the abuse, perhaps blaming the victim for wearing certain clothing. It is important to remember that abuse is never about love – and it is not normal. Abuse is always the fault of the abuser.

Fear and depression

Victims often feel afraid of their abuser and may feel afraid of other people, too. They may be scared to let anyone touch them – even a doctor. They may feel sad, angry and alone, and this can lead to depression.

Social problems

Sometimes, victims react to sexual abuse with **antisocial behaviour**, such as shoplifting or starting fires. Relationships may become difficult, because victims no longer trust other people. Activities that were once fun may now seem pointless.

Preoccupation with sex

Children who are sexually abused sometimes behave in a sexual way with other people. For example,

Victims of sexual abuse may wash themselves obsessively, to get rid of the deep feelings of shame they may feel.

they may kiss people on the mouth, when that behaviour is inappropriate. As adults, they may have many sexual partners because they think that this is the only way that someone will love them.

Physical impacts

Sexual abuse can cause physical injury, such as cuts and bruises. Rape can lead to unwanted pregnancy for girls and women. It can also lead to **sexually transmitted diseases** (STDs) or human immunodeficiency virus (**HIV**) infection. HIV is the virus that causes acquired immune deficiency syndrome (**AIDS**).

Self-harm

Victims of sexual abuse sometimes hate their own bodies. They may stop looking after themselves. They may start to abuse alcohol or other drugs. Some victims cut or burn themselves. Tragically, others commit suicide.

Running away from sexual abuse that is happening at home may be the only way that victims feel they can escape from it. But running away is scary and lonely – and it can be very dangerous.

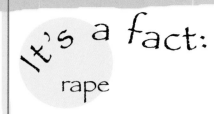

It's a fact:
rape

- Rape can result in pregnancy. Girls under the age of 15 are five times as likely to die during pregnancy and childbirth as women in their twenties.

Getting help

No one should have to suffer sexual abuse. It is important to remember that help is available for victims of sexual abuse. (See Getting Help, page 38.)

Chapter 5: *Neglect*

Neglect is a form of abuse. It occurs when someone fails to look after the basic needs of a person for whom they are responsible. This may be a caregiver neglecting an elderly or ill person, or a person with disabilities, or a parent neglecting a child.

What is neglect?

If children are to grow into healthy adults, their parents or other caregivers must take responsibility for their physical and emotional needs. The consequences for a neglected child are serious – and can last a lifetime.

Physical needs

A child's most basic physical need is for a balanced, healthy diet. Children also need a warm, dry, clean and safe place to live and sleep. Clean clothes that are suitable for the weather are also important.

Good hygiene helps children stay healthy, as does access to adequate medical and dental care. Children need fresh air and exercise, balanced with plenty of rest. Proper supervision helps to keep children safe. Parents should always know where their children are going and with whom,

Home should be a safe haven for children, and the place where their emotional and physical needs are met.

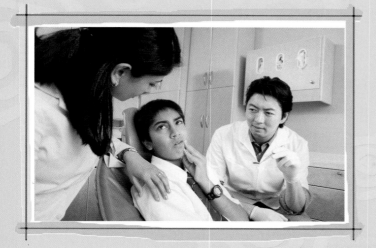

and when they will be home again. Adults also need to impose reasonable rules of behaviour for their children.

Emotional needs

A loving and caring home life is essential for children to develop into responsible adults with healthy self-esteem. When a parent shows affection and spends time with a child, the child knows that he or she is loved. If a parent or caregiver claims to love a child but does not show it, the child will not feel loved – and this is emotional neglect.

Adults who respect children – by listening to what they have to say and speaking to them respectfully – help them to develop self-worth. Giving praise and encouragement helps young people feel valued and encourages them to succeed.

Education is essential for people to play a full part in the world. Parents have an important role in teaching children right from wrong and giving appropriate discipline, if necessary.

In focus: wants versus needs

Should children be given everything they want, such as a new computer or the latest electronic gadget? Some people think so. However, good parenting is not about satisfying children's 'wants' but about fulfilling their needs.

CASE STUDY

After Leila's mother separated from Leila's father, she had a string of boyfriends. She often left 11-year-old Leila to look after her much younger brother, Adam. One time, Leila's mother left the children at home for an entire week while she went on a holiday with her latest boyfriend. She left Leila a small amount of money and told her to 'be good' and to take care of Adam. When a shopkeeper caught Leila stealing food from a local shop, he called the police.

What are the effects of neglect?

Neglect can affect children's physical and emotional development. Without proper physical care, they may become ill. Without emotional care, they feel unloved and unimportant. Over time, they may feel unworthy of love and attention, and this can affect not only how they feel about themselves, but their future relationships. Many experts believe that the effects of neglect may last longer than the effects of other forms of abuse, including physical and sexual abuse.

Hunting through rubbish bins to find other people's leftovers is one way that some victims of neglect cope with being hungry. But eating old food is embarrassing and humiliating. It tastes bad, and it can also cause stomach pain, diarrhoea and vomiting.

Physical effects

Children who are neglected may suffer from poor health. They may get lots of colds or **infections**. They may have poor hygiene, too: they may be dirty, or have bad breath and **body odour**. Their clothes may be dirty, old or scruffy. They may feel tired all the time, which can make it hard for them to concentrate or do well at school.

Some neglected children get very hungry, and they may steal food, or money for food from other people. Some children even have to search through rubbish bins to find something to eat.

Emotional effects

Neglected children often have very low self-esteem. Because they feel unloved, they do not know how to love or care for themselves. This can make it hard for

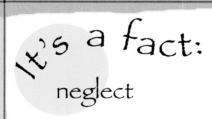

It's a fact:

neglect

- According to the National Society for the Prevention of Cruelty to Children, in the UK in 2003-2004, nearly 13,000 children were at risk of harm from neglect.

CASE STUDY

Eleven-year-old Chris doesn't have any friends. He usually stays away from other children at school and home, because they are mean to him. They call him names like 'Stinky'. Chris knows that his hand-me-down clothes are dirty. They are too big for him, too. But his parents never buy Chris new clothes and, if Chris puts his clothes out to be washed, they just get left in a pile on the floor. Chris knows that other kids make fun of him. He is really lonely, but he would rather be lonely than be called names and laughed at.

them to make friends – and they often withdraw from other people or from activities that should normally be fun.

Children who are neglected may become very depressed. Sometimes, they become dependent on other people – even on the person who is neglecting them. Lack of confidence can make it very hard for them to make their own way in the world.

Getting help

No one should have to suffer neglect. It is important to know that help is available for victims of neglect. (See Getting Help, page 38.)

Chapter 6: *Getting help*

All forms of abuse – emotional, physical or sexual abuse, or neglect – are terrible. Even after the abuse has stopped, the effects can last a long time. No one asks to be abused – and no one deserves it.

Recognizing abuse

Abuse can be very frightening. It may seem impossible to stop it. However, help and support are available for all victims of abuse. No one has to stay in an abusive situation. To bring abuse to an end, a victim must first recognize that abuse is happening and then tell someone about it.

Victims of abuse can find it hard to recognize that they are being abused. Abuse may be all they have ever known – so this behaviour seems 'normal' to them. Some abusers tell their victims that they 'love them', or that they 'are helping them'. Abusers may claim that the abuse is 'just a game'. Statements like these can make victims feel very confused.

Some abusers try to give their victims money or presents to make them feel 'loved' and to stop them from speaking out about abuse.

When people know their rights, and understand their physical and emotional needs (see page 6), they can more easily recognize abuse.

Hard to speak out

Speaking out about abuse can be difficult. Some victims are too afraid to talk to anyone, because their abuser may have threatened to hurt them if they do. Victims may also fear that they will not be believed or helped. They may worry that they will get into trouble. They may not want their abuser to get into trouble either, especially if that person is a family member.

Abuse is never the victim's fault. Even so, victims of abuse may feel embarrassed, guilty or ashamed about being abused. Some victims feel that they are responsible for the abuse or that they deserved it. They keep quiet because they think they will be blamed.

If someone is being abused by a family member, others in the family may know what is going on – but may not step in to help. They may be too ashamed or frightened to confront the abuser, so they ignore the abuse instead. However, if abuse is to be stopped, it is vital that someone speaks out – loud and clear.

Victims of abuse do not need to suffer in silence. Talking to someone might seem too scary – but it can be a life-saver.

Speaking out

Abusers will do anything they can to keep their victims from speaking out about the abuse. Abusers may threaten to hurt the victims or people they care about. An abuser may tell a child that no one will believe his or her claims of abuse. However, speaking out is the most important thing a victim of abuse can do. Reaching out to a trusted relative, teacher, counsellor or other person is a huge step on the path towards ending abuse, and towards ending fear, worry and pain.

No one has the right to abuse other people. Victims of abuse never deserve to be abused. Abuse is always the fault

A trusted friend can be a great source of help and support when someone decides they need to speak out about abuse or neglect.

of the abuser, not the victim – no matter what the abuser says. It is important to remember that there are always people who care and who can help. Victims of abuse do not have to stay quiet and suffer the pain alone.

Talking about abuse is difficult. If a victim of abuse does not speak out, this does not mean that he or she is weak or accepts the abuse. Victims often speak out when they are able, or when it feels safe. It is never too late to tell someone, but the sooner victims out, the sooner the abuse can be stopped.

Some victims live with abuse for a long time. They may then reach a point when they cannot cope with it any longer. They may find that they are unable to eat, think or sleep anymore. If they are abused by a family member, they may reach a point when they are too afraid to return home. They may also worry that the abuser will go on to hurt someone else. This often prompts the victim to take their courage in their hands and tell someone about the abuse.

Sometimes, another person, such as a friend or a teacher, may suspect that someone is being abused. The trusted friend or adult may be able to encourage the victim to open up about what has happened. That person may even have experienced abuse themselves and may help the victim to realize that he or she is not alone. Eventually, the friend may convince the victim to get help and support.

In focus: finding a voice

People who are abused sometimes reveal the abuse unconsciously. It may accidentally 'slip out', perhaps in a classroom discussion or in a casual conversation with a friend. At other times, people decide consciously that the time has come to speak out about the abuse.

Victims may feel very alone, but there is always someone who cares about them who can help to put a stop to abuse and neglect.

Victims may find it easier to phone a helpline to find the support they need to bring abuse to an end.

Where to find help

When victims of abuse decide to speak out, they should talk to someone they know they can trust. This may be a parent or other relative, or a good friend. It may be a teacher, or a school nurse or counsellor. People can also talk to a doctor, a religious leader or a police officer.

There are several trustworthy organizations, such as ChildLine in the UK and ChildHelp in the United States, that offer support to victims of abuse. They have free telephone or email helplines, and trained staff to understand and help. More information about these organizations is available on the Internet or in local phone directories. (See page 47 for a list of child abuse organizations and helplines.)

Sometimes, victims of abuse need to speak to more than one person in order to get the best possible help they can. If a victim tells someone about abuse, and nothing is done within a week, he or she should tell someone else – and keep telling until someone provides the help that the victim needs and deserves.

What happens next?

Some people worry about reporting child abuse in case it makes things worse for the victim, or the victim's family is broken up. Some abused children may be taken away from their family, but this only happens if it is too dangerous for the child to stay at home, or if there is no other choice.

When someone reports child abuse, government child protection agencies offer professional help. Trained staff talk to all the professional people who know the child, such as the child's teacher or doctor. They also talk to the child's family. If the child has been physically or sexually abused, they tell the police.

The child protection agency staff work hard to find out exactly what happened to the victim, and whether it is likely to happen again. They then work out a plan for how best to help the child and keep him or her safe. Decisions are also made about what will happen to the abuser.

Victims of abuse should always remember that the abuse is not their fault. What happens to the abuser is not their responsibility either. People who have been abused are strong and brave – not only for surviving the abuse, but also for telling someone about it. Their strength will help them to recover from the abuse, too.

Child support agencies can work with the whole family to make sure that a young person gets the help they need.

Chapter 7: *Recovery from abuse*

Emotional, physical and sexual abuse and neglect, are very hard to experience. The effects of abuse are deeply damaging to victims, and can last for years. However, victims can – and do – recover from abuse. Once the victim feels able to speak out, help is available to bring the abuse to an end. No one has to suffer abuse alone.

No one forgets abuse and neglect but, with help, victims can go on to be happy and lead successful lives.

In focus: *safety from abuse*

To stay safe and to help to bring abuse to an end, victims should:

- Stay safe, as far as they can (for example, try not to be alone with the abuser or go anywhere that abuse might happen).
- Trust that if something does not feel right, it is not right.
- Remember that the abuse is not their fault.
- Tell someone they trust about the abuse, or contact a child abuse helpline.
- If they feel in immediate danger, phone the police (dial 999 in the UK).

A new life

No one asks to be abused. No one deserves to be abused either. Victims of abuse have a lot of strength inside them. This helps them to deal with the abuse, while it is happening. It also helps them to recover from the abuse. Hundreds of thousands of people are abused every year, all over the world. Many of these abuse victims succeed in putting the abuse behind them and move on to lead full and happy lives.

CASE STUDY

Jane was neglected by her parents, and physically and sexually abused by her older brother, for two years. She felt very lonely, and soon became depressed. She was always tired and she could not keep up with her schoolwork. She had no friends, and life seemed pointless.

Jane thought that no one cared about her. One day, she felt desperate. She heard about an organization to help children like her. She was scared, but she dialled the helpline number. The person who answered was very kind and listened carefully as Jane spoke. Jane felt that the woman believed her and wanted to help. She convinced Jane to talk to her teacher at school.

Jane was surprised at how much her teacher cared about her. He reassured Jane that she was not alone. He explained that he would need to talk to a child protection agency, and he told her the steps the officials would take to help her.

A year later, Jane feels much better. Her family life has started to improve. The abuse has stopped. Jane feels more confident, and she has made some new friends. Jane will never forget – but she knows now that she can put the abuse behind her.

When a victim's old life of abuse comes to an end, a new and happier life can begin to flourish.

Glossary

AIDS Acquired immune deficiency syndrome, the final stage of HIV infection.

antisocial behaviour Actions that may hurt other people, such as telling lies or stealing.

body odour An unpleasant smell on someone's body, caused by sweating. People may have body odour because they are unable to wash or bathe.

child protection agency A government organization that can give professional support to victims of abuse.

coerce To force someone to do something.

comply To do what someone asks or wants of you.

contradictory Two or more things that are opposite from each other,

corporal punishment Physical punishment, for example by hitting someone.

corrupt When someone uses their position of authority or power to make somone do something bad.

depression A mental health problem which causes someone to feel very unhappy and think that there is no hope.

disability An illness, injury or condition that makes it hard to do some things that other people do. Some people have physical disabilities and others have learning disabilities.

discipline To punish people, or to teach them how to behave in a certain way.

domestic violence Emotional or physical violence that happens between two adults who live together.

emotional abuse An attack on someone's feelings, often through words.

ethnic minority A group of people who come from a different background to most of the people who live in a country.

explicit Very clear, obvious or detailed.

exploitation When someone unfairly uses or forces someone else to do something for them.

HIV Human immunodeficiency virus, the virus that causes AIDS.

humiliate To make someone feel ashamed and embarrassed.

infection An illness caused by a virus or bacteria.

intimidate To frighten someone, often to make them do something.

isolate To keep someone away from other people or things.

neglect When someone fails to look after the basic needs of a person for whom they are responsible.

paedophile Someone who is sexually attracted to children.

physical abuse An attack on someone's body, perhaps causing an injury.

poison To make someone ill, or kill them, by giving them substances that are poisonous.

pornography Words, films or pictures that are sexually explicit.

prostitute Someone who engages in sexual activity for money.

puncture To make a small hole, often with a sharp object or sometimes with teeth.

rejected Unwanted, unacceptable or unloved.

self-esteem Belief in our own value and abilities.

self-harm When someone hurts their own body in some way on purpose, such as cutting themselves.

sexual abuse When someone makes someone else get involved with sexual activity against their will.

sexually transmitted diseases (STDs) Diseases passed on through sexual contact, such as chlamydia, genital warts and herpes.

stress Emotional or psychological pressure or strain.

suicide When someone ends their own life on purpose.

vulnerable When it is easy for someone to be harmed in some way.

Further information

Books to read

Pete Sanders, *Dealing with Bullying - Choices and Decisions* (Franklin Watts, 2007)
Pete Sanders and Steve Myers, *Violent Feelings - Choices and Decisions* (Franklin Watts, 2007)
Sol Gordon, *All Families are Different* (Prometheus Books, 2000)
Adam Hibbert, *Children's Rights* (Franklin Watts, 2003)

Telephone helplines

ChildLine
A free helpline that young people in the UK can call to talk about any problems.
Telephone helpline: 0800 1111
Website address: **www.childline.org.uk/**

National Society for the Prevention of Cruelty to Children (NSPCC)
This charity runs a free child protection hotline which is staffed by counsellors who are all trained child protection officers. They offer advice and can take action to protect children at risk of abuse.
Telephone helpline: 0808 800 5000.
Website address: **www.nspcc.org.uk**
Email: **help@nspcc.org.uk**

National Domestic Violence Helpline
A free helpline run in partnership between Women's Aid and Refuge.
Telephone helpline: 0800 2000 247

Helpful websites

www.there4me.com
Online resources from the NSPCC aimed at young people aged 12-16 and covering subjects such as abuse, bullying and self-harm.

www.worriedneed2talk.org.uk
A website run by the NSPCC designed to give young people information about services and people that are there to help them. The subjects covered on the website include violence, abuse, neglect, family problems and bullying.

www.donthideit.com
A website with real life stories about young people who have experienced bullying, abuse and neglect. There is also help and advice for all forms of abuse.

www.youngminds.org.uk/
The website of a national charity that aims to improve young people's mental health. It includes information on and sources of help for bullying, abuse and neglect.

www.thehideout.org.uk/
The website of a national charity that aims to offer help, information and support to children and young people who are experiencing domestic violence.

Index

Page numbers in **bold** indicate pictures.